Day Trading for Beginners

How to Generate Consistent, Predictable Income Without Taking Big Risks, Even if You're a Complete Beginner

Greg Middleton

Table of Contents

Introduction

We currently live in a world that is dominated by entrepreneurship, profit, and exciting lifestyles, so it makes perfect sense that people are so eager to find new and innovative ways to make an income. Let's face it, life is simply becoming more expensive by the day, and unless you have a secret fortune, or you were born into obscene wealth, or you created the next billion-dollar innovation, having an additional source of income—which is profitable and does not require a (too) high bill of start-up costs and expenses—is crucial to most households.

Now, while day trading can have a substantial influence on your income, there are so many differing opinions out there which can make it super confusing to understand what it's about. How does one start day trading? How much capital do you need? Are you supposed to have hundreds of thousands of dollars lying around to be able to get yourself started? Who do you really trust for information? How do you know what is the right stock to invest in? And what the heck are margins anyway? These are the major inquiries that many people have in the back of their minds when considering investing in the stock market and (more specifically) day trading. But the biggest question that most people should be asking is, "How do I manage such high risk?"

Let's be honest, day trading is not for the faint of heart. If you decide to go into this venture, you'll need to treat it like a full-time 9 to 5 job (or at least a night shift job after your day job). This is the first mistake that people make when they decide to day trade. One thing that I will tell you is, the successful day traders are the ones who are dedicating time, effort, and skill towards this endeavor. And this should apply in any circumstance whereby a person decides to learn something new. Think about when you were in high school or college. You didn't just wake up one morning and suddenly know how to solve algebraic equations. It took time, practice, failing, trying again, practicing again, being patient with yourself, and most importantly—time!

It is a bit unfortunate that we live in a world where people think everything should just come so easily, and that you should be able to understand and learn something and become a master at it overnight. That will just simply never happen. We can blame the media for this. Even as I write this, I am thinking of those advertisements where people make day trading look like such a passive activity that you just do, by the way, on your phone. So, while we're going on this adventure together learning about day trading, the stock market, the history of exchanges, and all the other factors that culminate into this trifecta of transactions, remember that this is a learning curve.

One of the most important things to constantly emphasize is the risk that you're taking with your money. Unfortunately, not every investment turns into gold in the end. Whether you're investing in the very short-term or making a longer-term investment, there is always a risk that something will negatively affect the outcome of your investment. If you can make peace with that and accept it early on, then you're already on the right path. With any financial or monetary transaction, it's always good to try and depersonalize your interaction with it.

A good thing to begin doing is to look at day trading as though you're starting a business. Irrespective of what type of business you're starting, the principles are still the same. You need capital to begin the operations of the business, you're going to run into expenses and running costs, sometimes you're going to incur losses that you'll need to recover, you need to manage your accounts and cash flow, you need to sell and market yourself, you have to be patient and put in a lot of effort to get good results, you need to be consistent, *and most importantly, you need to make a profit*! The list really does go on; for any entrepreneurs reading this, you probably know all about it and then some. And if you, for a second, think that running a business doesn't come with any risks whatsoever, then you are so far off the mark.

This is what we're here to explore. How to get yourself started. We're not talking about the super-complicated stuff that the pros are doing; that's something we'd need to graduate towards down the line. But it's important to start somewhere, and there is value in explaining difficult concepts in a language that everybody can understand. The most important thing that you should take away from reading this book is that day trading is not a get rich quick scheme. If you want a get rich quick scheme, go and enter the lottery or become a criminal because in either of those scenarios, you may get a big reward, but it will be short lived, and you'll just be in a worse position than when you started. Here, we are all about integrity, fairness, dedication, and education. Unfortunately, there is so much misinformation and poor education about a lot of things in the world, and day trading is not immune to it. So, it is important to educate yourself just for the purpose of understanding exactly what you *should* be doing and what the process is supposed to feel like.

Let's go on a little journey together and learn how to make money and manage risk.

Chapter 1:

Day Trading - What's it all About?

Do you remember an ancient time when people utilized the barter system to exchange goods and services? It's so weird to think that once upon a time, money just didn't exist. But in the 21st century, money most certainly does exist. When people exchange goods or services, they generally use some form of money. Of course, there are a small number of people in the modern world that still use the barter system, but, in essence, people still trade with each other every single day. In its most rudimentary format, the word 'trade' means, "the act or process of buying, selling, or exchanging commodities, at either wholesale or retail, within a country or between counties," (Dictionary.com, n.d.) and this also involves "stocks, bonds, or currency".

The words 'buying', 'selling', and 'exchanging' are paramount to understanding exactly what we're trying to achieve here. What are you buying, selling, or exchanging? Anything! Crude oil, currency, commodities, minerals, food products, stocks (or a group of stocks), shares in a company, or any other instruments. Earlier I mentioned that investing is like running a business; and when you're running a business, your aim is always to buy something at the best possible price and then (hopefully) sell it at a higher price. The difference between the amount that you spent to purchase the item and the amount that you received after selling the item could be a profit or a loss.

In general, whenever people are trading on the stock market, they put money in, and hold that money as stock for an extended period—i.e., multiple years. During that time, the money is hopefully growing and increasing in value. After the time has lapsed, the investor may retrieve their investment with a bit more than what they initially put in. This would be considered a profit. Even if the investor only put in $100 and then after the period got out $150, that means they made a $50 profit. It doesn't sound like a lot, but that is the core principle of business. Buy low and sell high.

Short-term versus long-term investment. Day trading is an example of short-term investment—and in this case, a very short-term investment that lasts no longer than 24 hours. When you're trading within a 24-hour period, the same rules will still apply. Buy an instrument at a low price, check the value of that instrument throughout the day, then sell it when it has gained more value, and keep your money if you are profitable.

The first thing to do is get yourself setup and trained. There are many programs out there that can teach all the intricacies of how day trading works and specific details about all the different concepts. Training means that you're going to be in a phase where you're learning and experimenting. Training is important because day trading is a high-risk and volatile environment. There are constantly elements that affect different trades, and it is always unpredictable what will happen in the market throughout the course of your trading window. People require training because they need to learn how to manage risk and to objectively see if they can make more profits than losses.

As a beginner, it is important to identify the low-risk entries which have more potential to give you a bigger win. Even if your first trade is $1000 and you only sell at $1150, you still made a profit of $150. $150 worth of profit for five days of the week; you've already cashed in $750 in your pocket, just by aiming for the slower money.

It is important to constantly remind ourselves that every time we trade, we expose ourselves to a high level of risk. Therefore, the implementation of systems or setups can help manage your interactions. The volatility of day trading is something that can be to your advantage if you are working in a calculated way. If there are no rapid fluctuations, this defeats the point of day trading. Constant movement is a factor that determines how much you profit or lose. Most of the job description of a day trader is fulfilling the same requirements as somebody who manages risk for a living—whilst also maintaining a consistent output of profit over loss.

There are questions that you should ask yourself when you are a beginner. Do you have a comprehensive knowledge and understanding of the terminology? Are you going to adopt a proven profitable strategy, or will you design your own strategy? And most importantly, are you willing to put yourself through a simulator that would treat the trading as if you were using real money and real-life situations? Acquiring knowledge is the first important step. The knowledge is the theory behind the practice. A doctor doesn't just become a doctor without going to medical school first. This is the part that most people loathe because they think they can just make guesses and hope for the best.

Once you have answered these questions, you are well on your way to begin understanding the steps that you'll need to take to make utility out of this in a real-time scenario.

When it comes to trading, it is recommended that you research strategies that have been proven to be profitable. Of course, you can create your own strategy, but this can be a bit of a hindrance for a few reasons. You will need to test your strategy, see if it is profitable, refine it, re-apply it, and constantly work on it. And because it would be a novel strategy, there will be very limited resources out there to help you with undertaking a deep analysis of it. This can take months, and sometimes years, during which you would not be using real money.

When it comes to adopting a trading strategy, it is important to stick to one and really exhaust all the possible outcomes of it before deciding if it works for you. There are many people out there who make grand claims about having the best strategy, and it is your job to ensure that their claims are valid. This is where the transparency of a strategy is super important. Can this person provide bank statements to show their growth over the years? Is there a regulatory body that can confirm the legitimacy of this strategy? Are they open to scrutiny? If not, then you have your answer.

It is better to master an already existing strategy, and once you have more confidence, one can make customizations that suit the individual. Try to consistently practice one strategy before you decide if it is for you or not. It is not advised to dip your toes into different strategies. In other words, don't become a jack-of-all-trades but a master of none. How are you going to know if a strategy is fully profitable and effective if you aren't seeing it all the way to the end?

Know that you will never truly be ready to do any trading if you don't understand these theories. The way to practice is to use a trading simulator. This is computer software that replicates real-life stock market trading scenarios. Making use of a simulator allows you to test, practice, fail and learn whilst being in a controlled environment. It also has the added benefit of not trading with real money, thus allowing you to objectively understand and analyze your progress. I cannot stress enough how important it is to critically assess yourself and not assume that you'll know everything. You need to see, with cold hard facts, that you are ready to trade in the real world or if you still need practice. Make a concerted effort to practice daily.

Once you begin to see that you're making progress, start thinking about the tools that you will need to put the practice into the real world. The first important tool is a broker. A broker is an internet-based application that, "allows its clients to open and close positions using a digital platform". The important thing to remember about brokers is that not all brokers appeal to the same niche. Some other niches within the world of stock market investment (besides day trading) could be options trading and passive trading. A few brokers that you could consider, based on reviews, assessments, and general opinions are IG, eToro, and Plus500.

Something else to keep into consideration is how fast these brokers execute trades. Seconds literally matter when you're trading because in a matter of seconds, there could be a monumental change that could make a massive influence on your trading position in any given moment. If you were to slip up on a moment where there was a catch, you might have missed an opportunity, and ultimately that may have been the difference between a really good profit and a mediocre one, or a significant loss. For this reason, day traders should opt for a broker that gives them direct market access (DMA). As the term indicates, you get direct access to the services that can facilitate your trades, without the need for too much third-party intervention. Investment banks make use of "sophisticated electronic trading technology" because their trades are generally on behalf of their clients, and they work with higher volumes of money. As a retail trader, having this type of technology can help you with your operations.

A lot of people assume that all brokers offer direct market access, but they do not. Some brokers route the order to the market on your behalf, often combining your order with other clients' orders, and giving some customers priority over others—essentially acting as a middleman. Having a middleman means spending a few extra seconds, or minutes, communicating additional and redundant information in order to obtain a result. This will cost you time, and time (in this case) quite literally costs you money. Remember that, within seconds of any fluctuation, the position of that stock can change quite drastically, and if you are not there to capitalize on that fluctuation before the stock plummets, you could be in a situation where you lose out big time. If you want to be a successful day trader, you need to invest in a broker that works optimally and speedily. Never mind the situation of the hardware of your computer; you can have the most expensive computer in the world, but if the broker software is slow, lagging, or requires third-party action, this is going to cost you time that you may not have. So, you need to eradicate the middleman and get yourself a broker that will ensure that you'll have direct market access (DMA). With direct market access, you can sell your stock as quickly as you want without waiting for your broker.

While it is good to have a broker, also consider that they charge a fee for their services. These are called commissions. While the word "commission" may sound nice for a salesperson, it is not so nice when you have to physically pay for those commissions yourself. As a day trader, you will be making so many transactions, and those commissions will add up if you're not considering your options. There are two ways in which brokers will charge commissions, either per-share or per-trade. You need to decide which option will work for you, and that will depend on the size of your position.

'Per-share' pricing is the most popular and most common with day trading brokers. You only pay $5.00 per trade, and when you reach a certain average trade, $5 per trade becomes almost negligible. Your decision about which broker you will want to make use of should not solely depend on the commission fees that they charge. Cheaper doesn't always mean better, and there are many brokers that will offer you cheaper commissions, but their infrastructure might not fully meet the needs of your day trading requirements. There are some brokers who get paid for "directing their order flow" (warriortrading.com,n.d.) and this can impair your result showing time.

Once you've decided on a broker that suits all your needs and requirements, it's time to invest in the next tool, which is a stock scanner. The reason you need a stock scanner is because it forms the basis of helping you to decide which stock you need to purchase at any given moment in time. Most beginners struggle to even decide on which type of stock to buy. Again, we are not making guesses and just throwing random arrows into the sky and hoping that we hit a cloud. This is where you need a device that scans the markets in real time, also known as a stock scanner—this is not to be confused with a stock screener which searches the market for certain trading trends and then provides you with a list of static stock stats—usually from the previous day.

Think of a stock scanner as the live stream and the stock screener as the recap. You can see how having a good stock scanner can be beneficial for a day trader who wishes to trade within very short timeframes. If you see live, immediate, current, and up-to-date information about the stocks that you wish to trade with, it helps you to make informed decisions on the go. This can be useful to mitigate some of your decisions and ensure that you are not missing any important information or updates that could affect the value of your stock and ultimately the value of your profit (or even your loss).

In order for you to understand which stocks are the right ones to trade, you need to have that information available in a reliable format. Check which stocks are moving as a result of a catalyst and where there is a high relative volume. Anytime a stock is moving and in action, it is called a stock-in-play, and these are the ones that we need to be aiming for. They generally have a better chance of displaying trends throughout the day, and this can make them more predictable. And what is better than having a predictable stock? Well, nothing really. The benefit of having a good stock scanner can really increase your chances of generating consistent profit and just generally being able to trade with ease and predictability. Trade-Ideas has received glowing reviews from acclaimed websites like TopTradeReviews.com, so this is a good tool to use in the sea of competitors out there.

The final tool that you'll need in your arsenal is a charting platform. The challenge with charting platforms is that so many of them experience difficulty with meeting the highly-intensive demands of day traders. In this regard, eSignal and Robinhood have been listed as two of the best charting platforms that day traders make use of.

So... you've assessed the various tools that you will require to become a successful day trader and acquired those. More importantly, you've made sure that you are practicing on a trading simulator, deducing critical analytics about your performance and overall skill level, and you are (at least) 95% confident about your abilities—honestly and objectively. Remember, if at this point you've still been lying to yourself (or cheating), and you do not have cold hard facts to substantiate your abilities, you will most certainly run into grave errors, and nobody wants that. The odds of you risking real money and winning—whilst having no experience, knowledge and/or strategy—are like finding a unicorn. In other words, they're non-existent, and if you do win, please don't count on that luck to carry you further into the future.

At this point, you will need to make some practical steps towards turning this into a reality. You will need to open a brokerage account with one of the abovementioned brokers (like Plus500) and start transferring money into that brokerage account. Once you've done that, create a written plan that you adhere to and review every morning. This plan essentially tells you how you're going to conduct your trades and deal with your interactions. You will then have a list (called a 'watchlist') where you write down which trades are the ones you'll be paying attention to. Get into the trading and make sure you are following your trading plan and not deviating to it. The point of the trading plan and the watchlist are to help you maintain continuity and discipline, and to keep a reference point every time you run into a curveball or an exciting new stock becomes available. Then make sure you're reviewing your trades at the end of each day. Check for any mistakes, where anything could have gone wrong, take screen captures of the charts and try to analyze some of the information.

Now this may seem like a simple list of things to do, but some people really struggle to maintain even simple tasks. Part of the reason as to why they struggle is that emotions and psychology can really trigger people and drive them to forgetting all the rules (more on this later).

For first-time traders, take it slow and don't rush throughout your process. Remember that making brash decisions is not advisable. If you dive in head-first and trade with too much opening size, you might run into problems later when you potentially experience a loss. Make it easy for yourself and try to become comfortable. Trading with real money comes with an emotional and psychological element as well.

Remember, this is your own money that you've worked for, so if something happens to it, you will most definitely be upset, and you might crack under the pressure. Once you've cracked under the pressure and you're desperate—GAME OVER! However, with experience (and some desensitization) these feelings will gradually subside. And don't put all your soldiers in the frontline. Make sure you keep money aside so that you can continue living and trading more as you become more skilled. Imagine being a first-time trader, throwing all your money into this venture, trying to score a big profit and buy an obscene amount of shares only to lose it and have nothing to invest in anymore. It's counterintuitive and just plain careless.

A new trader needs to make their main focus about mitigating losses. If you can learn how to lose less, your wins can become bigger and accumulate over time. People tend to focus on trying to win big all the time, and maybe with the right strategy you could win big all the time, but the success rate of day traders (especially beginner traders) is super slim, so don't try to aim for big wins all the time. It's better to gradually earn $5000 whilst having lost about $2000 during the process than to suddenly win $5000 and then lose it within seconds after that. The way that you can manage this is by setting stop losses promptly as you enter a position. The worst habit to get into is constantly moving orders around because of your worry about what might happen during the trade. If you understand everything about the trade *before* you get into the trade, it can help with managing your trade and keeping your mindset balanced.

Chapter 2:

Let's Talk About Charts

In the world of day trading, the most important tool for the trader is the stock chart. This will be your greatest friend, unless you are not careful... then it may feel like your worst enemy. There is so much terminology involved with trading. Let's start with a basic definition of Technical Analysis, and then move into the different levels of chart analysis.

Technical Analysis

Technical Analysis is the visual and mathematical study of stock trading charts. The purpose of tech analysis is to use past market data (up to very recent data) in order to forecast the future market direction, primarily using stock prices and trading volume. Carefully using these charts will allow keen-eyed day traders the insight to know when a buying or selling opportunity has just arrived, and give them the confidence to pull the trigger on a trade.

It is always very easy for someone to conduct a post-trade analysis. Like they say, "hindsight is always

20/20". When you study a huge market change after the fact, it can be quite easy to pinpoint the signs leading up to it. For example, for the five years leading up the dotcom crash of 2000, the tech industry was booming. This is now referred to as the dot-com bubble, because it burst quite terrifically in March 2000. But were there signs beforehand? Of course there were. Emerging tech IPOs were getting funded without any real experience or product, just hype. This included funding for problems that didn't even exist! There were fierce IT recruiting wars, trying to fill tech positions that kept expanding out of control. And if we study the stock trading charts of that period, there are all kinds of hints that prices were overvalued and a crash was overdue.

These are the signs that a day trader needs to recognize *before* a crash occurs, or at least near the very beginning of one. Remember, day traders can make plenty of money on a crash (selling stock), just as well as they can make money buying stock before a stock upsurge. Let's have a close look at the information we can glean from stock charts.

Stock Chart Types

Bar Charts

Bar charts are the most commonly-used chart type for day traders. They contain four essential pieces of information: the opening price for the day, the closing price, the daily high and the daily low. For each day's trading history, a vertical line represents the price fluctuations of a particular stock for that day. If a bar is red, that indicates a loss over the day's trading, so the closing price is lower than the opening price. If the line is black, it indicates a daily profit for that stock. A little tick to the left indicates the opening price; a tick to the right indicates the closing price. A series of these bars in a row shows the daily price ranges over a period of time—from weeks to years—and is an excellent visual aid, giving a trader an immediate feel for the direction and volume of that stock's trading.

Candlestick Charts

Candlestick charts present the exact same information as the Bar chart, but in a slightly different format. The candle, or "real body" of a day's candlestick chart indicates the difference between the opening and closing price. If the real body is white, the stock has gained in value over the day; a red body indicates the price fell. The thin line—also known as the 'shadow'—

that extends above and below the real body indicates the low and high trading values for the day.

Line Charts

Some day traders only consider the closing price of a stock, so they prefer not to look at all the information contained in a bar or candlestick chart. For those traders, all they need is one data point per day (closing price), so these points are simply joined into a line over time, resulting in a line that rises and falls with the daily close.

Point and Figure Charts

A Point and Figure (P&F) chart looks quite different again; in this case, only price is considered, while the passage of time is completely disregarded. A column of Xs shows that price is increasing, while a column of Os indicates a decrease in price. One column may only contain either Xs or Os, and there are certain rules which govern when to start a new column—each time a change in column occurs, it indicates a new trend.

When this system is used, certain patterns emerge that can help a trader discern whether a breakout has occurred. In other words, they can see if a stock is suddenly heading in a new direction, which can trigger a buy or sell order, depending on the direction of the breakout.

Parts of a Stock Chart

Using a live view of a real stock will be the very best way to really dive in and see what it is we're talking about here. I am not endorsed by any stock websites; there are a number of free stock chart websites, including:

- TradingView.com
- TDAmeritrade.com
- StockCharts.com
- StockRover.com
- Ca.Finance.Yahoo.com
- Google.com/finance

These, and many more charting websites, offer free and subscription memberships, allowing users to view real-time daily stock charts. Depending on membership level, users can make trades and fully operate their day-trading business using one or more of these trading sites.

If you have a computer handy, please join me in visiting a free stock chart website. Let's try TradingView.com. If you navigate to this URL in your browser, you'll see a large search bar on the center left. Click on "Search markets here" and for the purposes of this discussion, go ahead and click on the Apple stock, which has a ticker name of AAPL—you should see it on the first page. Once the page loads, you will be looking at a real-time representation of the current stock value and stock history of Apple, Inc!

1. Chart identification

   If you look up in the top-left corner, you'll see the chart is labeled with the stock name, Apple Inc, with the Apple icon above it, and its ticker name, AAPL. In the same area you can see that the trading index is the NASDAQ.

2. Summary Key

   The number directly below the stock name (Apple) is the current sale price of the stock.

3. Time Period

   At the bottom left of the chart you will see different time increments of 1D, 5D, 1M, 3M… all the way to All. If you click on 'All' you will see the complete trading history of Apple stock, all the way from its founding in December, 1980. It was first sold at $22 per share, but since then, Apple stock has split five times. On a split-adjusted basis, the IPO share price was actually 10 cents, which is exactly what this chart shows if you zoom in to the very first day of trading!

Now click on the time period '1D' which stands for one-day. The chart will now show you the trading that is being conducted in real-time, starting this morning at the time the NASDAQ opened for business. On the right-hand side of the chart you will see a new candlestick is being drawn as you look at it, each passing minute. The candlesticks are red for cost decrease, and green for cost increase, though these default colors can easily be changed.

4. Moving Averages

Please look at the top left of the chart: above the Apple Inc — NASDAQ — TradingView line you will see different menu items. If you click on *Indicators*, a page will popup, with a Search bar; type in "Moving Average", and click on Moving Average (MA) in the list. You will see a new line appear on your chart, and a new entry will appear just below the Summary Key: if you hover over the line that begins with 'MA' you will see a gear wheel icon. Clicking on this icon allows you to change the type of MA; try changing the Length to 5 and then 50 day MA. The Moving Average line on a stock chart is a very helpful tool that helps to identify support and resistance. MAs, support and resistance will be discussed in greater detail later in the chapter.

5. Volume

    Along the bottom of the chart, below the stock price candlesticks, you will see a row of bars that indicate the sales volume for that particular period of time. A red column indicates that more stocks were sold during that period than were purchased; a green column indicates the opposite. Sales volumes are a very important indicator of market momentum.

6. Trade Range

    The main candlestick trading chart depicts the trading activity for the selected time period. If you click '1Y'on the bottom left, you will have selected to view the past year of trading. There will be 260 candles on the screen, one for every work day (weekends don't count). Using the mouse scroll wheel, you can zoom in to the very last day (today—assuming it's a work day).

7. Earnings & Revenue, Dividends, Stock Splits

    Still looking at the 1Y stock chart, look at the bottom of the chart. Superimposed on the Volume indicators, along the X-axis, you will see different colored shapes with the letters 'E',

'D', and 'S'. Clicking on a 'E' shape will display the essential information in the Earnings and Revenue report for that period. Clicking on 'D' will display basic information about the dividend that was paid out on that date. 'S' indicates a stock split; the date and the split ratio is displayed here. All of this information might be considered part of fundamental analysis rather than technical analysis, but these 3 elements should be held in consideration when making trading decisions, even when day trading.

Support and Resistance

Considering support and resistance can be a very strong element in the decision-making process that is day trading. Let's draw some lines on this chart and use them to determine support & resistance. If you use the same AAPL stock trading chart we have been considering, click on the 1Y Time Period at the bottom left. You'll notice that a peak (high point) occurred in September 2021. Now look at the far left column, where you will see some tools. The second item from the top looks like a diagonal line. Click on that tool, and draw a horizontal line through the high point you noticed in September 2021, and extend that horizontal line all the way to the right, clicking just after today's date. Now, draw another horizontal line that passes through the high points that occurred in Dec '21 and March '22. The lower line can be considered a line of Support, while the upper line is a line of Resistance. The upper line of resistance is fairly obvious, as this is a price point that has not as yet been exceeded, although it has been approached (known as being 'tested') a couple times, particularly in March of '22. The lower line of support was at one time (in September of '21) a high price point, but when the price broke through that point of resistance in November of '21, it became a level of support.

At the time of writing this, I can see that today, on May 2, 2022, the daily trading price of Apple has reduced down to that very same level of support, so as a day trader this is quite a significant day. I cannot safely say at this moment whether the trading line will break through the line of support (in which case I should sell the stock short to make a profit) or if it will bounce off the line of support and return in the upwards direction (in which case I should buy stock to make a profit on increasing stock prices). From your vantage point sometime in the future, you can see which decision I should make right now to make lots of money from this stock, though I do not have the benefit of hindsight. I will go out on a limb and say that without conducting any fundamental analysis, as a day trader I believe that right now, on May 2, 2022, would be an excellent time to buy Apple!

We have just done some technical analysis of the Apple Trading chart. While not an exact science, support and resistance lines can help us make very important buying or selling decisions.

Channels

Channels are very similar to the horizontal support and resistance lines we just reviewed, except they are drawn on a diagonal. Using the same Apple trading chart, let's zoom out a bit by clicking on the 5Y time period. With this view, you can clearly see that in March of 2020, Apple stock hit a bit of a low point, then began marching consistently upwards.

Let's draw some more lines and see what technical analysis tells us about this chart view. First, right-click on the 2 lines you already drew, then select *Remove* from the list of options. This will prevent your chart from getting too messy. Now, select the Line tool again from the far left, and carefully draw a line from the peak in Aug '20 to the peak at Jan '22. You'll notice a couple candlesticks that peak over the linc, but we'll ignore those for now; the bulk of the trades are below this line. Now draw a second line that extends from the low point in Sep '20 to the low point in March '22. If you don't like where you've drawn the line, you can always hover over the end of the line and then click and drag the line to a slightly different location.

You have now drawn a channel. In some ways, this is more informative than simple horizontal support and resistance lines. Now, those channel lines represent the ongoing upwards trend of Apple for nearly the past year. The price has clearly fluctuated within that channel, but so far this channel has largely encompassed the entire trading direction of Apple, and there is little evidence that this trend will change. Do you see now why I think May 2, 2022 is an excellent time to buy Apple stock? This point in time is known as an Entry Point, where a day trader should consider very seriously whether now might be the time to make that important purchase decision.

A very experienced trader could look at this same chart, and consider every time the stock price reached the support line (lower line) of the channel, they would buy, and each time it reaches the resistance line (upper line) they would sell, thus maximizing their potential profits. This is known as Swing Trading, and can be very profitable—but it takes a lot of practice, experience and discipline.

Moving Averages

Moving Averages (MAs) are another very important technical indicator for traders. Let's draw another line on this chart and find out how they work. First, we'll remove the two channel trend lines by right-clicking and selecting *Remove*. Now, do you still have the Moving Average line you drew when we were going over chart identification? If not, click on *Indicators* at the top of the chart, and then search for Moving Average, and select it. This indicator is now shown beneath the Summary Key at the top left. Hover over the MA entry, and click on the *Gear* icon. Click on the *Inputs* tab, and change the default *Length* of 9 days to 50 days, and click OK. Now, click on the 5Y Time Period at the bottom left. You'll notice something pretty interesting: the 50-day Moving Average acts like a very strong support line. Again, this gives us a strong indication that May 2, 2022 will prove to be a key support point, and as a day trader I would expect the stock to rally. This should prove to be an excellent entry point.

There are many, many other trading indicators in use by professional day traders, some of which will come in handy for you as you become more experienced in the trade. I highly recommend that you spend lots of time with the available online trading tools, just experimenting and conducting practice trades until you feel very confident with them.

Chapter 3:

Trading Discipline

There are millions of traders out there in the world who each have their own strategy. The most important thing to remember is that you are trading using a strategy and context that works for you and is comprehensible to you. There is no point using strategies and theories that aren't working for and that you simply have no understanding of.

There is also value in learning patience. Because there are so many traders out there, some people have a tendency to do what we call in the industry "over-trading". This is what happens when someone makes more than ten trades throughout a 24-hour period. Now, if you over-trade, that means you'll have increased the number of commissions per trade. Let's say you are trading at $100 per trade and each trade is costing you $5 in commission fees. You then decide to make 20 trades. You've already spent $100 in commission fees. That means, whatever profit you make will have a $100 deduction at the end of it (just in the commission fees alone). Add another 20 trades and you're already at $200… and so on and so forth. Your broker will be super happy to take their commission, but your wallet will not be happy giving them.

You're always going to have moments where you lose money on trades, it's just part of the game, especially because of slippage. An example of slippage is when you go to sell at $5 and then the market gets filled at $4.90. In this scenario, you've lost 10 cents. If you have 1,000 shares and you're losing 10 cents per 1000 shares, you've lost $100. If you have 10,000, you'll lose $1000. One thousand dollars is a lot of money to be losing because of slightly careless mistakes. And while the potential for slippage is inevitable, it is also a risk that can be mitigated through appropriate application of your strategy. You should only be exposing yourself to risk if you have proven—to yourself and through cross-referencing, fact checking, and practice—that your strategy is suitable for trading.

It's important for you to be very specific about what types of stocks you are willing to trade. You do not need to utilize quantitative barometers to make your decisions. Use a strategy that works for you and that is easy to learn. Pattern-based strategies have been quite big in the industry of trading. Of course, you should try to be sure that you're trading with a company that isn't specifically trying to destroy the world or infringe on human rights, but mostly what you should focus on is the patterns. Patterns are effective because a lot of people are watching them. Even if you are wrong 40% of the time, you can still make an income by relying on patterns in conjunction with effective risk management techniques.

The current market is dominated by Algorithmic High Frequency Trading. Algorithmic means computers, and computers are generally smarter than human beings. This means, for the most part, you'll be trading against computers. One thing about trading against a computer is that it has thousands of outcomes that have been built into its DNA and its software. Have you ever tried to play a game of chess with a computer? Well, there's your answer.

There is no way that a human being would be able to outsmart a machine that knows all the moves before you do. And if 60% of the market is being conducted by Algorithmic High Frequency Trading, there is no point engaging with this trade. But that's only 60%. The remainder is a small handful of stocks each day that are going to be trading on such heavy retail volume that we can overpower and take control over them. It is important to make sure you focus on that remaining 40% which constitutes mostly retail trading. These stocks are typically gapping up on earnings. PR is related to this. They have a ton of retail interest and retail volume. So, that means regular traders like you and I stand a chance and can buy these stocks. By doing this, we can compete with the computer systems.

When price action is plotted on the chart, the patterns are formed. Make use of candlestick charts. Each candlestick represents a period of time, and you can choose the timeframe of the chart that you're looking at—daily, hourly, 5 minute or 1-minute charts. Candlesticks can tell us a great deal about the general trend of a stock. Large body candles are very bullish. Candles with a big red body means that the open was high and the close was low. This is a pretty good indication of 'bearishness' in the market. Just by learning how to read candlesticks, we can begin to generate an opinion about the general attitude of the stock.

Find an explanation about which patterns are the best in terms of candlestick patterns, and that will give you a more thorough understanding about this. Patterns dominated by computers are meaningless.

When it comes to pattern trading, the more traders that use these patterns, the better they will work. The more people that recognize that this is a line in the sand where they should buy, the more people are going to buy at that point, which will make the stock move up faster. The more buyers, the quicker the stock will move.

This is the type of thing that makes me so happy to share pattern-based trading because it helps traders to become more profitable. Also, the more people that use this trading strategy the better it will work. And the reason why it works is because this small handful of stocks are being very well watched each day. Lots of people are watching them and waiting for a breakout. That ascending wedge.

Pattern trading does not work on all stocks. It only works on stocks that have high relative volume. Some stocks, like Apple, have millions of trades per day, while others will have significantly less. High total volume could throw us off. Pattern breakout trading is also a way to trade. This can also be called momentum trading: wanting to buy a stock while it's running and not during the phase of consolidation. When trading with pattern breakouts or momentum trading, the amount of time that you are exposed is critical. Instead of impulse buying, hold and then wait, just wait for the breakout. Take your money and conclude your trading for the day and claim your profits. Also, consider that there will be an apex point.

With reversal patterns, we're looking for clear confirmation that the pattern is beginning to reverse. This is usually the first candle to make a new high. If you're not careful and you buy a stock when it's selling, this is called catching a falling knife.

Setting stops can be very important while day trading. You need to draw a line in the sand where you decide it's time to get out. You can be a successful trader but part of being a successful trader is dealing with a controlled amount of losses. So, that means I must've found a way to be a really good loser, but losing gracefully is just as important as winning, because you need to know when to walk away. Ask yourself these questions: is the stock moving up? Are we still trending up? What is the low of the last five-minute candle and have we broken that low? (Because if we broke the low of the last five-minute candle in an uptrend, then the trend may be starting to change). We have to follow the charts. It's really hard to take a huge loss, so it's important to mitigate that by setting stops. Rather take the smaller losses and then come back the next day to continue trading.

Stock trends with the market. Keep in mind that stocks will trend with the overall market, unless they have a reason not to. This is a big part of algorithmic trading. If the market is running and these stocks are running too, then that's fine—we just need to make sure that we're trading stocks that are moving because they have a reason to move. A quick sell-off because of bad news, a lot of people are going to watch it because of the bottom bounce.

Retail Traders versus Institutional Traders. Retail traders—that's all of us, you and me, the ordinary people that are trading. Regular traders, part-time traders, full-time traders, but we're not working for a firm and we're not managing other people's money. We are a small percentage of the volume that exists within the market. The majority of the volume within the market is institutional traders. Institutional traders represent large amounts of capital. They are trading the accounts of their clients. They can be extremely aggressive and have huge positions. They include banks, hedge funds, and mutual funds. We have to be careful and make sure we're not getting on the wrong side of institutional traders. For now, just recognize that what we want to do is, instead of finding institutional traders, find out where the retail traders are hanging out today and trade with them. Focus where everyone else is focused. Can we day-trade a stock like Apple? These are slow-moving stocks and they're dominated by institutional traders, and algorithmic traders; this means, in general, that they're going to be more challenging to day-trade. How do we find what the retail traders are focused on? How do we find that cool place in the playground? By watching our scanners (or gappers). Stocks that are gapping up the most are the stocks that retail traders are watching. It's good to be in touch with social media, stock twits, Twitter and what stocks are trending. If you're trading completely on your own, you're off in the corner of the playground, you're not in touch with what other people are doing, inevitably, you're going to make it really hard for yourself. You just don't know where the activity is.

When doing day trading, something that is important is being organized and maintaining structure. Remember when I said earlier, that doing day trading is like running a business or working a full-time job? When you work a full-time job you obviously clock in and clock out, you attend to daily duties and fulfill a job description. This is the same when you're doing day trading. You need to wake up every morning and have a strict routine that you adhere to stringently—don't deviate from it. You need to allocate time to different activities. You need to do some pre-market scanning. Check for a Stock-in-Play watch list for that day. Sit down at a specific time (maybe 10:00 am) and begin your trades for the day. Start slow, then become aggressive during the course of the day, and then slow down again as you're about to conclude your trades. I cannot stress how important it is to review your trades and all your transactions at the end of each trading day. Remember, you're running a business and developing skills for long-term success and entrepreneurship. All successful business people review their work and their progress and generate analytics and/or conclusions about their work and how they can improve going forward. This is a continuous journey of learning and adapting. Try to avoid pre-market trading.

Let's think about the psychology market. If you make $1000 by 11:00 am, what do you think you're going to do? A lot of people will walk away, take their profits and conclude their trading for the day. (Remember, this is all in line with your targets and your strategy. Your routine could say, your trading hours are from 10:00 am to 2:00 pm, but if your routine and strategy says, "In addition to these hours, if I am a position where I reach a profit of $1000, then I need to stop for the day and essentially cut my working hours shorter—if I reach the $1000 target well before 2:00 pm. But if during these trading hours, I don't reach the $1000 target by 2:00 pm, then I need to stop anyway, because this is my strategy and my routine and I must maintain discipline, tomorrow is another day). Some traders will lose $1000 by 11:00 am and then continue to fight out the market and try to force a win out of desperation. Remember, you're not making emotional decisions—this will be explained in more detail in the chapter about (e)motions. And because there will, by default, always be traders that are trading desperately and aggressively trying to make back their losses, the market will be saturated by midday. That means midday trading is dominated by traders that have lost in the morning and are aggressively trying to make it back. That causes a lot of volatility, but not in the good way that we are looking for. This causes stocks to shoot up and shoot down because people are going in and out of market orders. (More amateur traders!)

And this then leads to the next chapter about all the factors that influence the market.

Chapter 4:

External Market Factors

The stock market is quite a busy place and there is constantly a stream of activity that surrounds the stock market. To better understand why it fluctuates so much, it's important to understand some basic principles and factors that can affect our trade decisions. The stock market has a general ebb and flow about it. There are times where the overall market is very choppy. It is advisable for us that we adjust our risk based on the market's conditions. If the market is choppy and we're having trouble generating a profit, then it's better to scale back the risk. Reduce the exposure so that our losses aren't too severe. Then, when the market starts to pick up, and we've got a hot streak, we can start to lean in a little bit and get heavier with our trading.

The stock market has been around for at least 200 years. One of the first stock markets opened in London (it is called the London Stock Exchange) in 1773, and subsequent to that—in 1792—the first stock market in the United States opened in Philadelphia. This market paved the way for the New York Stock Exchange (NYSE) on Wall Street. There is a lot of history behind the trading industry; this gives you a pretty good indication of the level of experience and expertise that you're dealing with here. But with a lot of expertise and experience comes a lot of complications and sensitivity to conditions – if you're asking yourself why there is so much volatility in the stock market, this context will probably help you to understand better.

So, let's scale this back a notch. The basis of economics and finance is supply and demand. Simply put, if a commodity is highly demanded, then the price will increase to reflect that demand. If there is more supply than there is demand, then the price will have to decrease. And if there is less supply and more demand, then the price will increase again. These are the fundamental basics of economics. So, why is this important when it comes to the stock market, and more specifically day trading? Supply and demand are important because it can help you make more informed decisions about your trades.

Say for example, there is a hot new stock that nobody is talking about, but you can see for yourself that this stock will have a lot of potential for growth. In that scenario, there will be a pretty substantial supply of that stock meaning you'll be able to buy it at the best possible price, as there won't be too many people jumping the queue for it. But once that stock reaches a point where it has gained so much popularity and thousands of people are placing orders, you'll be in a unique position where you can sell your stock for a much higher price because you already own it, and now there is less supply.

In order for companies to remain profitable, they need to increase their price when the demand is high and the supply is low so that they can maintain the same amount of money they would have made if the stock was in more supply and they could charge smaller amounts of money and receive higher volumes. It's all about the numbers. If you sell 100 shares at $1 each, your revenue will be $100, but if you only have one share left to sell, then you can rapidly inflate that price to $100 for that one share in order to maintain your $100 revenue. And it's always important to remember that a company will review their prices depending on their current conditions and their needs at that given point in time. The best skill to have as a day trader is the ability to make predictions—this takes time, deep analysis, and technical understanding, and the ability to extract information from charts and stock screeners. It can also help if you can remember the basic principles of supply and demand in all your day trading interactions and considerations. Again, it's not about buying the hottest stock right now, it's about sticking to a strategy, and slowly and consecutively accumulating your profits. Again, don't focus on that big $10,000 win for today. Rather accumulate $10,000 over the course of 100 days of earning $100 per day. Slow money is always better than no money at all.

Supply and demand are not exclusively influencing stock prices and the overall stock market. There are so many other external factors that could influence how your trade is going to fluctuate throughout the day. If you watch the news and you stay informed, there could be developments surrounding the company that could negatively or positively impact the value of their stocks and people's willingness to invest or divest. If you're a company that produces tinned food on a global scale (or even a multinational scale) you could run into problems of food insecurity. And because there is a lack of certainty that affects your production, this could present a big risk to investors and ultimately cause them to withdraw or retract their investment. This would then cause the demand of the investment to go down. If the demand for the investment is plummeting, that means prices will also plummet and this could have a negative effect on the value of your shares (since you are actually "the investor").

Sometimes, though, it's not even as serious as food insecurity; sometimes, there are just better brands within the same industry or the same scope who are selling more products and are able to sell more shares and make more money. This is just part of the competitive nature of entrepreneurship and capitalism. This part of the decision is really about personal choice. You know, if there is a new clothing company that's now starting up and you're not too sure if you should buy their shares or if you should buy H&M's shares, you're probably going to stick with the more predictable option of buying H&M's shares. This is not to say that H&M's value will stay consistent forever, but at least for right now, it's more predictable than the newer competitors who don't have as much exposure and trust from the public.

It is also important to look at the financial statements of the company. Besides the share price, see if they have any assets or liabilities. What is the ratio between their assets and their liabilities? Are their liabilities potentially exceeding their assets? Then possibly, this might not be a company to make such a sensitive investment in. When looking at their financials, examine how the company is doing in terms of profit from one year to another. Public companies should be releasing their financial statements (which is not to get confused with bank statements or other confidential information) on a bi-annually or quarterly basis. This is important because it gives very recent and up-to-date information about the financial state of the company, which can help to formulate an objective opinion about your investment.

If you want to know who the CEO of the company is, this can also shape your decision-making process. Is the CEO a person who is embroiled in any scandal? Have they acted ethically throughout their time as a CEO (or even throughout the time that they have built themselves to become the CEO)? Is the CEO of the company somebody that is trusted by the public or do people feel dubious and unsure about this CEO? Regardless of who the CEO is or isn't, if they ever experience a moment where they make questionable decisions or they aren't trusted, it will affect the perception of the company, and this can have further effects that trickle down.

The other factor of this part of the conversation is the ethical discussion. Ethics are very important to me when it comes to choosing who I invest in. We currently live in a world—whether you like it or not—

that seems to be falling apart and burning around us. It is important to make sure that you're not investing in a company that is contributing to the destruction of the world. We're not trying to make a quick buck here, we're trying to invest in our future, and just because a company may have billions of dollars right now and you can potentially make a lot of money from them in the short term, it would be quite useless to have a lot of money while there is complete instability in the world and you can't even enjoy it. It's counterintuitive, in my opinion. Make sure the companies you are investing in (even though it's only for the day) are companies that do not make morally objectionable decisions—like human trafficking, exploitation, pollution, and destruction of ecosystems to name a few—and that you're being conscious about your own decisions. Because every cent that you invest towards any company (ethical or not) helps that company to grow, advance and contribute progress towards their standing. Remember, if a company has gained notoriety or infamy because of a deeply unethical history or other social issues, this does have an effect on you whether you can see it right now or not. And if they go down, they'll take you down with them—i.e., your investment—that might incur a serious and avoidable loss.

There are also times where companies endure harsh events. Sometimes it's within their control, but for the most part, things can just go disastrously wrong and there is nothing they can do to stop it. And it's not always an issue of infringing on human rights and/or being unethical. Think about the company Boeing. This is a company that has a pretty respectable reputation considering that it is the main reason why a lot of people can travel to other countries across the oceans—a respectable reputation for innovative and engineering genius that has given opportunities to so many other flight companies, thus creating more success for other companies and opening doors for people to create micro-industries within this big industry of aviation. Then all of a sudden, there was a Boeing-affiliated airline (Ethiopian Airlines) that crashed as a result of the plane malfunctioning. This crash injured and killed so many civilians. And of course, when bad news like this strikes, people's immediate response is to pull themselves away and withdraw their involvement with the company. It's not the people's fault that the plane crashed, but once this harm to their reputation was done, it had further impacts down the line.

Information is power, but it's what you do with that information that is critical. If you are able to disseminate information and use that information to inform your decisions, then you're already at a good place. Remember, if you are making an effort to stay informed and up-to-date with all the developments that are occurring in the world, it can help you to constantly stay ahead of the curve. Having a proactive mindset is highly crucial when it comes to day trading or even just investing in the stock market.

Let's take this Russia-Ukraine tension in 2022. There are people who definitely would have been able to predict that these tensions would turn into something substantial and impactful. Why? Because they were following the news and doing research on a daily basis, understanding the economics of the country, and recognizing that the events and standing of all countries affect other countries. If you are a country that exports petroleum (like Libya) and you're now embroiled in a war, it will affect how you choose to export petroleum to other countries. You can, as a country, decide to restrict your petroleum exports to other countries that are not expressing devotion to and allyship with your country. This can then affect so many other things down the line. Gas prices increase, which means retail prices increase, and then that means everything that people consume becomes expensive—and this can put strain on the economy, and so on and so forth. But the bottom line is, if this country is somehow connected to a company that you invest in, there will be a point where that company will feel the brunt and the wrath of these negative effects, and then you as an investor will also ultimately feel it. Staying informed and keeping yourself proactive can help you make proactive decisions which can protect your investment and yourself way ahead of time. Because the worst thing is trying to make a decision after the stock prices have become negatively affected, and this decision that you're making is not a profitable one; or you find yourself in a desperate position to pull out of a trade and you still make an uninformed decision that could have just been avoided.

Keep yourself informed and remember that context is always important. No matter what you do, you will be so happy if you just have the knowledge ahead of time all the time. And it's not to say that you need to go on a deep history dive and understand how each and every single company works, and what all the secrets are of economics and what are all the rules and regulations of each country and who the president of each country and what is their story and are they popular among the people... etc... that's not necessary. It's just important to perform a deep dive into the companies that you are currently investing in on a daily basis. Because part of your day trading strategy could be that you'll buy and sell shares repeatedly from the same company because you know and trust the predictability of that company.

The only way to stay ahead of the curve is to make sure that when you have discovered that company that facilitates consistent outputs for you that you're not going to run into any problems down the line. Identify red flags within the company. Are there any social causes that they are contributing towards? How do they spend all their extra money? Who are the directors and major stakeholders associated with? Do they pay their employees fairly? Is the company's business model sustainable or does it rely heavily on unsustainable resources? (And when you're asking this particular question, remember to try and be fair—maybe the company produces a lot of plastic to package their products, but they encourage people to recycle and perhaps they have a program where they could collect all their plastic output and they try to mitigate it themselves—it's an odd example but okay...)

Remember, it's your money, so it's your own choice where it ends up. There is no reason to invest in stocks in a company if you are not interested in that company. Of course some people are not particularly interested in what the company does, who they are, what their story is; they just want to do the trade, look at the numbers, check the patterns and get out of the market. And this is fine—ultimately at the end of the day it's all about personal preference and personal choice, and you won't always have time and energy to do such deep research about each stock that you're trading and the entire root of that stock—but keeping yourself informed and acquiring knowledge about the intricacies of business and economics and how they relate to humans on the planet can be a good edge to have.

Chapter 5:

The (e)motions

Part of the thing that goes pear-shaped in the world of day trading is the emotional and psychological impact that it has on an individual. It's so easy to say that human beings can just detach themselves from financially strenuous situations, when in reality, people simply hate wasting or losing. However, the other side of this coin is true as well. People also love winning or gaining.

So, day trading is all about depersonalizing the results that occur from your interactions. If you win or lose, do not have an emotional reaction after that. Do not think that you're on a winning streak and try to go for more gold, and definitely do not start making desperate decisions because you're now on a losing streak. When you win, stop for the day and keep the profits that you've made. That's the secret; it is really that simple. Remember, you're a day trader. That means that you'll wake up the next morning and you'll have another opportunity to make some more trading decisions. And the same applies for when you lose—lose gracefully, accept your loss, and be done for the day. Again, you will have another day to start the recovery process for the loss that you incurred today. There is a reason why you practiced so many times on the simulator, and why you made contingencies by not putting all your money into the trade of that day.

To become a successful trader requires knowledge, practice, and skill, but it mostly requires discipline and focus. Having a clear mind 24/7 is the key to making levelheaded decisions. Of course, this exists in every area of life, not just day trading. Making emotional decisions is a big no-no in the world of day trading. And not just when you make bad decisions, but also when you make good decisions too. Don't suddenly commit to something outside of your strategy just because of some exciting news or a catalyst event that doesn't apply to your strategy. People see a headline on the news like: "Activist investor has decided to take a stake in Apple Inc.," then their first reaction is to capitalize on this and try to buy thousands of shares because they're being opportunistic. If part of your trading strategy is to be opportunistic, then buy the thousands of shares, but if not, take a minute to evaluate that situation and decide for yourself if you really need thousands of shares right now—irrespective of Apple's latest development.

When trading, you need to learn how to make decisions for yourself that are both intuitive and well-informed. Being focused, calm, and maintaining composure is a highly valuable skill. Because trading is like multitasking whilst under stress and pressure. And when there is extreme stress and high pressure, it can put your body into fight, flight, or freeze mode. You can almost feel paralyzed in a state of indecision, and you start catastrophizing. This is when you need to realize that you may have bitten off more than you could chew and that you need to find a way to exit that situation before you make it worse or destroy yourself. The problem is that people do not realize how disturbing it could feel to make such big losses, especially if you had a pre-existing plan to avoid it. When you get into a losing streak, it can impair your judgment and cause you to feel demoralized.

Do not become complacent and think that you know everything. Do not think that you never need to refine your strategies and your skills. Ask yourself imperative questions like: "Does this fit into my trading strategy?" "If this trade goes pear-shaped, at what point do I stop?" "How much am I actually risking in this trade and is the reward worth the potential of the risk?" The minute that complacency kicks in, that is when you will very quickly be corrected for it. Making quick decisions is important, but keeping your mental health in check is what will maintain your ability to execute those good decisions.

Patience is a valuable tool in your arsenal of emotional preparation for trading. I consider myself to be a very patient person and I enjoy maintaining that patient disposition especially when I am dealing with money. Because the day trading market is specifically volatile by nature, the amount of activity that instantaneously occurs minute-by-minute adds to the volatility of the stock market. So, the stock market is already a volatile place in and of itself, but now when you add all the traders out there that are making crazy, reckless, and haphazard decisions, it heightens that volatility tenfold.

And remember, as day traders, we should thrive from volatility and not suffer from it. Learning how to be patient is important in any area of life but when it comes to how to trade your money, your patience is more important than ever.

Imagine this scenario: there is a stock that you're trading and suddenly there is a catalyst event that occurs, and it's going to affect your stock. The opportunistic response would be to quickly sell that stock and take your losses (depending on the severity of the situation of that stock, this might be the right move) but if this catalyst event is the first event in the series of more events that you'll predict throughout the day, then holding onto that stock and waiting until the second catalyst could be well worth your while. What do I mean by this? I mean that the market is likely going to change drastically throughout the course of the day. It may seem like a catalyst event that is bringing bad news at 11:00 am, but by 2:00 pm investors might have a completely inverted opinion of that stock and the value could shoot up, and then you can capitalize on an even bigger profit. You wouldn't know that if you just decided to sell when everybody else was panicking and you decided to join the panic train.

Having a proactive mindset rather than a reactive one is all about emotional state. If you maintain confidence that your strategy works and if you also aren't putting all your money on the line, then it makes it a lot easier for you to take a loss if you need to, and then your loss won't be so severe, and ultimately you can then continue to trade the next day.

People have this tendency to think that whatever situation they're in, it will be the last and only time that they'll be in this situation or it'll be the last time there will be certain opportunities. Aren't you creating future opportunities for yourself in a passive way already by building yourself up slowly? Volatility and high pressure should not be conflated with stress, panic, and desperation. Once you accept that the market is a volatile place, it can become easier to manage the pressure and the stakes. Also, once you accept that the market is highly unstable, you'll be more reluctant to trade with all your money in one go. If you don't trade with all your money each time, you'll feel a bit more confident about preempting losses because, again, your losses won't be excessive.

The emotional component of day trading is criminally underrated and if you choose to not manage that, you'll be putting yourself in a position where you'll have to feel, experience and deal with hard decisions without any preparation. In life, the most important thing is to have balance and moderation. The stock market is a risky place, and with high risk comes high tensions, that is the inevitability of it—whether it's something you feel comfortable with or not is what you'll discover as and when you engage with day trading.

If you can prepare your mind, learn how to breathe, maintain composure, stick to your strategy and not deviate or react or sway, then you're on the path to a good venture. Remember, day traders manage risk for a living, that's what we do, it's part of the game. If you can feel confident with having a 2:1 profit loss ratio, then it means you understand how business works. There are always running costs, there will always be a trade that trips you up and goes haywire. But if you're losing $1000 yet your general revenue stream is $10,000, and initial deposit was $2000, that still leaves you with $7000 to take home.

Do not let losses discourage you; learn to find lessons in each of those losses that you can apply to your future trading days. It'll help so much if you choose to see the learning as a journey and a foundation whereby you're acquiring knowledge and building up your wealth.

Remember, if you pocket $100 per day for 365 days a year for a period of 5 years, that could add up a value close to $200,000 ($180,000 to be exact). This is far better than risking $200,000 in one trade hoping that you won't lose it all.

Conclusion

People have been exchanging goods and services for centuries (and possibly even millennia). In the days before money was invented, human beings would do something called 'bartering'. This meant that they exchanged goods and services without the use of money. Over time, money became a part of our dialogue which meant any goods and services that were exchanged involved a monetary transaction, subsequent to this primitive idea of bartering. Of course, there are still communities that exist in our current world which implement more modern and sophisticated versions of bartering, but for the rest of us on the planet, money is the primary medium that measures how goods and services are exchanged. Money is earned through a variety of techniques, and depending on who you ask, money can then be saved or spent.

Whenever people spend money they're generally buying products or services, and there is always a value (or a cost) assigned to those products; and depending on what their motives are, they might sell that product at a later stage. Should they decide to proceed with selling said product, they will want to gain something that benefits them; i.e., profit. This is one of the cornerstones of running a business: exchanging goods and services with the aim of making money. If capitalism has taught us anything, it's that profit is the most important element of running a business and managing money. Even if you are not an entrepreneur, any person who earns a living understands why it is important to not lose money.

People who are business minded generally understand that making an income and finding new and innovative ways to continue making an income and investing is a never-ending priority. When it comes to making money (or even running a business) the task is a simple one: buy something at the best possible price and sell it at a higher price. And what is another word for buying and selling? Trading—more specifically, day trading. A trade is "the act or process of buying, selling, or exchanging commodities, at either wholesale or retail, within a country or between counties," (Definition of trade | Dictionary.com, n.d.) and this of course involves stocks, bonds, or currency.

Now, while day trading has been around since the 1970s—give or take—it is only in recent times that people have become more acutely aware of its existence. Think about the countless number of advertising campaigns that are seen on YouTube promoting new applications and platforms that promote that "big money fast" message about trading online. Now, this is what is generally known as speculative investing. People misconstrue day trading as this get-rich-quick scheme, when in reality, it is far more complex and requires a lot more patience, dedication, and proper education in order to turn into something fruitful.

Day trading is definitely not a get-rich-quick scheme... that's winning the lottery, or gambling—and if you approach day trading with the same mentality that you would approach gambling, then you've already lost the battle before you could even qualify to enter the war battlefield. You aren't even at the frontlines and you're not even in the trenches. You're far away, still at home.

"Nothing in life is easy and straightforward," a direct quote from... almost every motivational speaker out there. And although some of those motivational speakers only amount to a lot of energy to deal with, ultimately, they are right about that one thing. Especially if there is something in life that you want to understand, execute, and succeed in badly enough, it will not fall into your lap just by you simply wishing for it. This should go without saying, but you should always aim to work smarter and be hungry for learning in every area of your life.

The problem with today's society is that the majority of us want to achieve greatness just by believing that we deserve it, or believing that we are worthy simply because we dream of success. Success is not about a destination; it should be about a journey of consistency. You shouldn't be aiming exclusively to make money (although that is the point of all this) but you should approach this venture as though you were a long-term investor. Put yourself through the trenches, learn valuable information, and constantly apply yourself when it comes to trading.

Of course, you can make so much money and not have to adhere to a 9 to 5 schedule or work for a boss, but you can also use this as a time to learn all the tricks of the trade when it comes to investing. One thing about acquiring wealth is that you can utilize that wealth to foster positive changes in the world, but you can also use that wealth to create more wealth. And who doesn't want that?

If you play your cards right, and slowly build up your daily profits over a period of time, it will add up and you can have a pool of money that's at your disposal which you can use to invest in other things down the line. If you spend the first three years saving and accumulating money to the value of $100,000, you can then invest that $100,000 into a venture that can start making a further $100,000. Now, you're making double the amount and you can invest more, get higher returns on your investments, and it takes you a much shorter time to continue building up more capital to continue to invest. Investing and entrepreneurship are journeys that go hand-in-hand. The point is not to show off your money and become flashy, the point is to leave behind a legacy, even if the only thing you're leaving behind is the tools to teach others how to trade in this industry.

Some day traders really fall into the trap of making careless mistakes that can arise from egotistical approaches toward life. Don't be overconfident and jump into the deep end too soon. Train and put yourself through intensive real-life simulations. There are millions of combinations of moves and techniques that exist within the stock market. There is never a completely right or wrong answer that applies perfectly to any scenario. But if you are equipped and you have filled your mind with more knowledge than you think you can handle, you're already on a good path. Rather be an overachiever who is thirsty for knowledge, than be arrogant and think you're too good to be hitting the books. And for humans, being overconfident is one area of life that everybody can identify with and even empathize with.

Do not treat day trading like gambling in a casino. Gambling is hugely risky; and while day trading is also a high-risk environment, you still stand a higher chance of winning than gambling where there is virtually almost never a strategy. Of course, there are exceptions, but it is important to make educated guesses and decisions rather than shooting shots in the dark and hoping to aim and hit the jackpot. In other words, don't be speculative.

Remember to treat day trading as if you're running a business. Successful businesses operate because they have structure, strategy, and most importantly they keep themselves accountable for all the decisions that they make. They perform critical analysis and hold themselves to the highest possible standards. Make your life into something of a higher standard and put that energy into your venture. If you set higher standards for yourself, you will conduct your work and your trading in ways that are congruent with that standard. Be strict and don't bend your will to suit the journey of somebody else. Different strategies and techniques work for different people. It is not up to you to prove to somebody else that you can do things their way and execute it well.

Making money is just inherently a personal endeavor, so it's okay if your feelings become negatively affected by some of the choices that occur. Don't focus on that one loss and think it's going to be that way forever. Keep yourself active and maintain a structure. If there is a strategy that you keep trying and it doesn't work, move onto another one or make sure you are indeed making meaningful adjustments to the strategy. Put in the effort and the work to understand and to develop the knowledge, and apply your winning strategy!

References

Am I a Pattern Day Trader? Know the Day-Trading Margin Requirements | FINRA.org. (2022a). Finra.org. https://finra.org/investors/learn-to-invest/advanced-investing/day-trading-margin-requirements-know-rules

Chen, J. (2022a, April 12). *Stock Market.* Investopedia; Investopedia. https://investopedia.com/terms/s/stockmarket.asp

Hwang, I. (2021a, January 8). *A Brief History of the Stock Market.* SoFi; SoFi. https://sofi.com/learn/content/history-of-the-stock-market

O'Shea, A., & Davis, C. (2022a, March 2). *What Is the Stock Market and How Does It Work?* NerdWallet; NerdWallet. https://nerdwallet.com/article/investing/what-is-the-stock-market/

O'Shea, A., & Voigt, K. (2022a, February 18). *Definition: What Is Stock?* NerdWallet; NerdWallet.

https://nerdwallet.com/article/investing/what-is-a-stock

Reinkensmeyer, Blain (2022 Jan 10). *How to Read Stock Charts (2022 Ultimate Guide).* https://www.stocktrader.com/how-to-read-stock-charts

Schock, L. (n.d.-a). *Thinking of Day Trading? Know the Risks.* | Investor.gov. Investor.gov; Investor.gov. https://investor.gov/additional-resources/spotlight/directors-take/thinking-day-trading-know-risks

Made in the USA
Las Vegas, NV
23 February 2024